William Bolcom

T0085028

Fancy Tales

for Violin and Piano

Fancy Tales is found on Albany Records, Troy 959-60, by American Double: "The Bolcom Project"

ISBN 978-1-4234-7545-3

EDWARD B.
MARKS MUSIC
COMPANY

EXCLUSIVELY DISTRIBUTED BY

HAL•LEONARD®
CORPORATION

7777 W. BLUEMOUND RD. P.O. BOX 13819 MILWAUKEE, WI 53213

www.ebmarks.com
www.halleonard.com

Commissioned by the San Francisco Chamber Music Society
for Daniel and Michiko Kobialka

FANCY TALES

1. The Phantom-Sweetheart

"... shucks, her hair was so soft ..." - from *Weird Tales* (*ca.* 1950),
about a love affair with a vampire.

DURATION: ca. 18:00

WILLIAM BOLCOM
(1972)

For glossary of symbols see page 32.

© 1993 by Edward B. Marks Music Company wend Bolcom Music
International Copyright Secured   All Rights Reserved

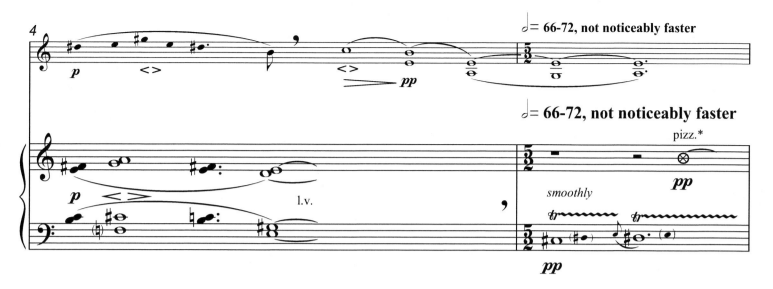

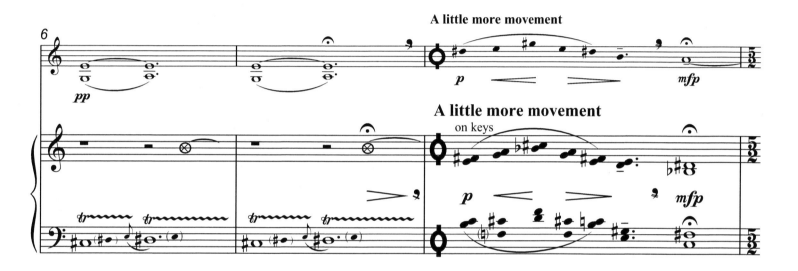

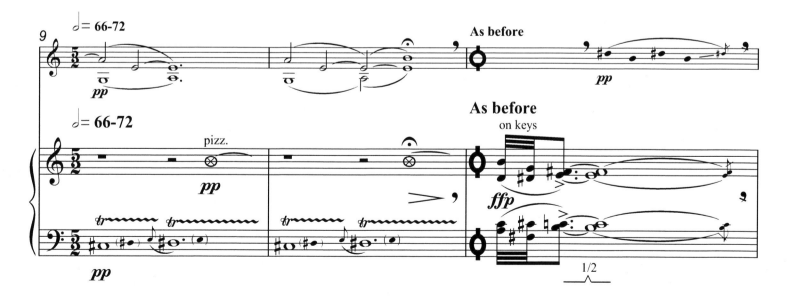

* inside the piano, pluck string of the pitch shown with fingernail

4

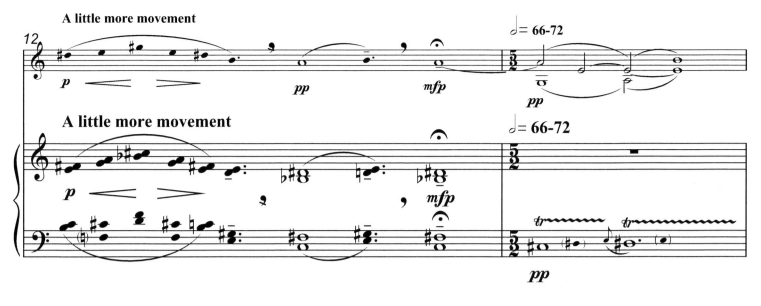

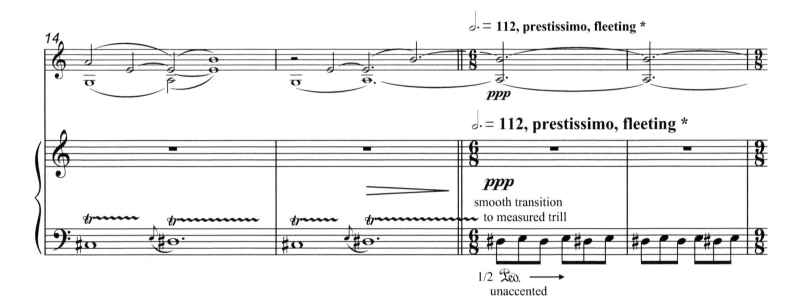

* It should never be absolutely certain in the listener's mind that the predominant meter in this
section is 6/8.

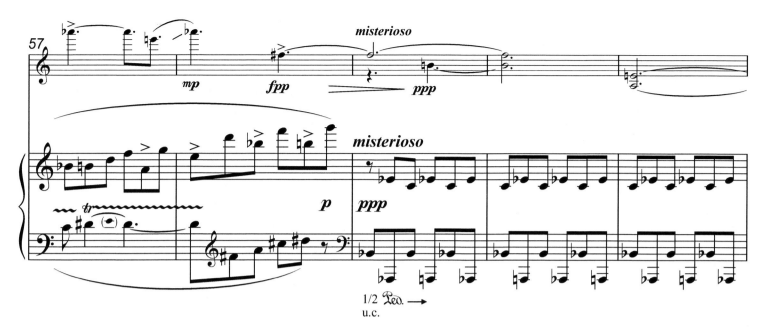

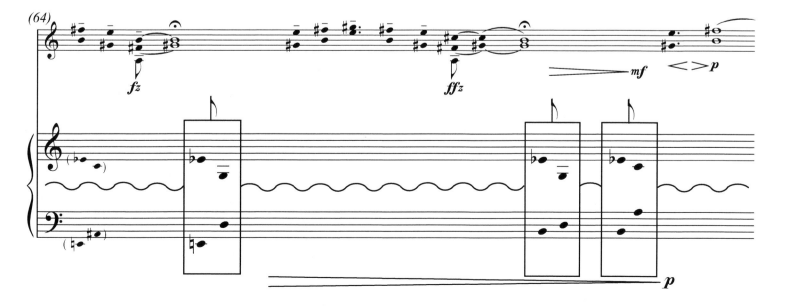

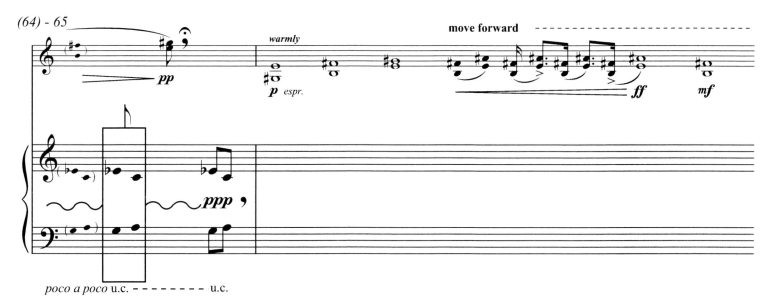

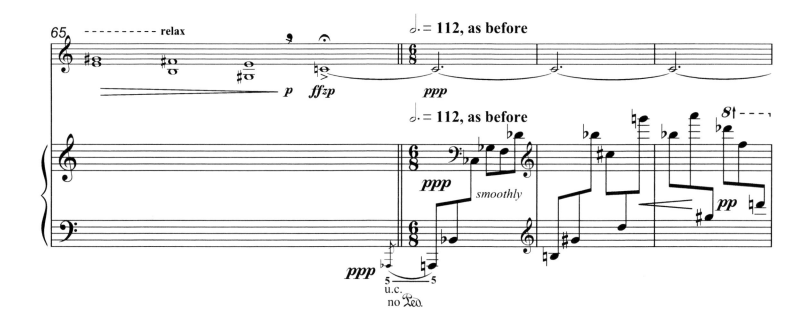

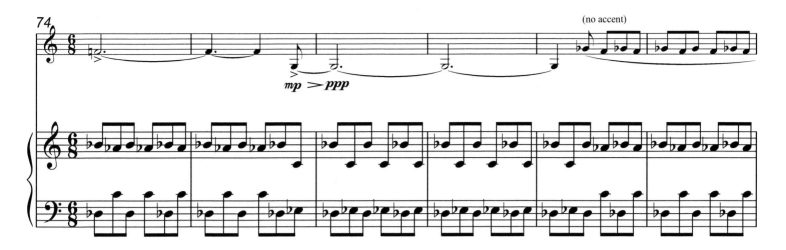

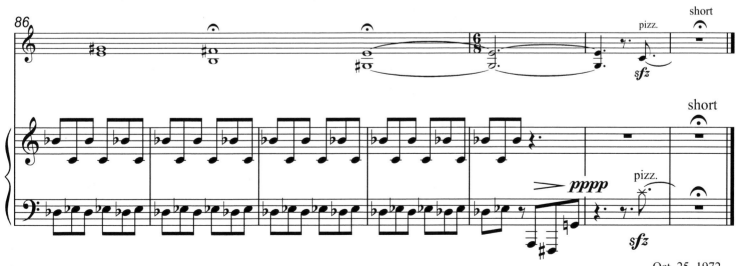

Oct. 25, 1972
New York City

2. The Centaurs in Flight

They run, swilling the cup of murder and revolt,
Toward the escarpment of their mountain hideout.
Fear hurtles them, they feel the scrape of Death's throat
Behind them, and they stink of lion-sweat and fright.

The hydra and the plotting lizard do not trip their hooves.
They trample across ravines, through hailstorms, over thick brake-
Ossa, Olympus, black Pelion will they overtake?
Just now the crest of the great cities heaves.

One of the herd looks back: whips his head back around,
And with a great whinny of savage fright
Leaps into the rolling stampede his brothers sound.

The gorgeous calm full moon does not make him bound
Ahead; it is the long shade the moon casts in the night,
The gigantic shadow of horrid Hercules bearing down.

    – "Fuite de Centaures," José Maria de Heredia, trans. W.B.

*fz is stronger than sf (which remains within the dynamic); sfz is stronger than fz.

* Bow and pluck with left hand simultaneously. Ossia: - bow only.

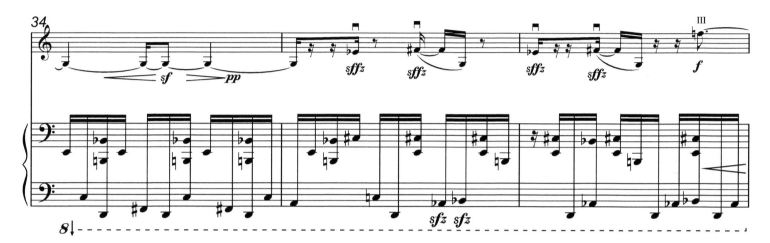

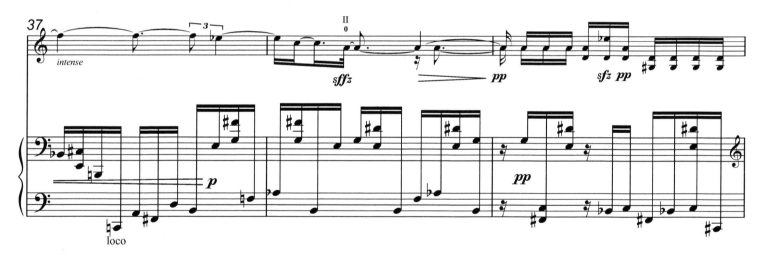

* circled dynamic = general dynamic exclusive of accents

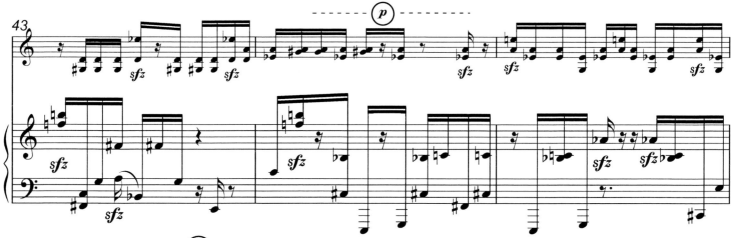

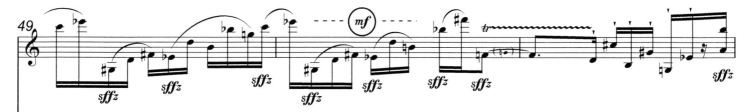

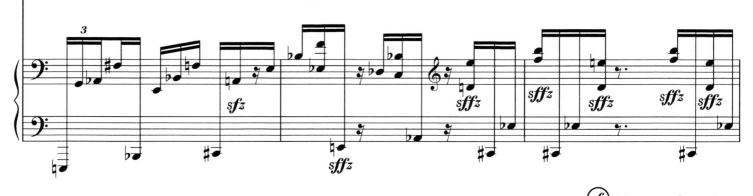

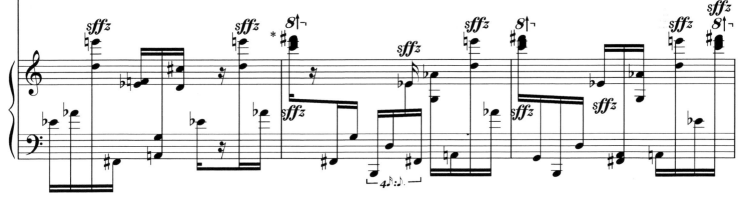

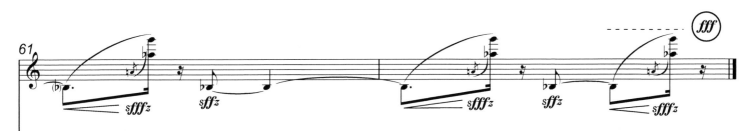

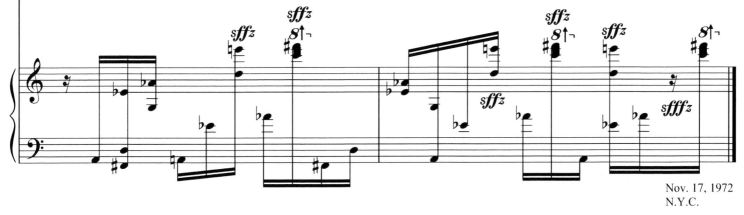

Nov. 17, 1972
N.Y.C.

**Very short pause
before 3.**

* ♯♩ = cluster, comprising as many chromatic notes as possible within the described interval.

3. The Dwarf's Serenade: Variations

(inspired by Pär Lagerkvist)

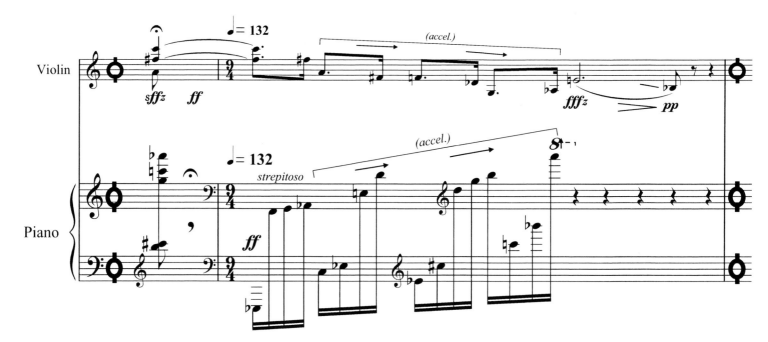

William Bolcom

Fancy Tales

for Violin and Piano

VIOLIN

Fancy Tales is found on Albany Records, Troy 959-60, by American Double: "The Bolcom Project"

ISBN 978-1-4234-7545-3

EXCLUSIVELY DISTRIBUTED BY

HAL•LEONARD® CORPORATION

7777 W. BLUEMOUND RD. P.O. BOX 13819 MILWAUKEE, WI 53213

www.ebmarks.com
www.halleonard.com

Commissioned by the San Francisco Chamber Music Society
for Daniel and Michiko Kobialka

FANCY TALES

1. The Phantom-Sweetheart

["... shucks, her hair was so soft ..." - from Weird Tales (*ca.* 1950)]

WILLIAM BOLCOM
(1972)

For glossary of symbols
see page 32 of Score.

* It should never be absolutely certain in the listener's mind that the predominant meter in this section is 6/8.

© 1993 by Edward B. Marks Music Company and Bolcom Music
International Copyright Secured   All Rights Reserved

4

2. The Centaurs in Flight

* ***fz*** is stronger than ***sf*** (which remains within the dynamic); ***sfz*** is stronger than ***fz***.

** Bow and pluck with left hand simultaneously. Ossia: 〄 - bow only.

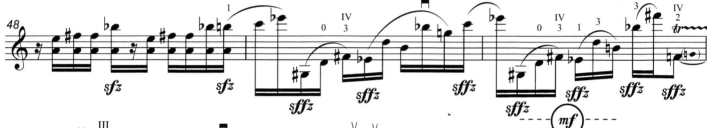

Very short
pause
before 3.

3. The Dwarf's Serenade: Variations

(inspired by Pär Lagerkvist)

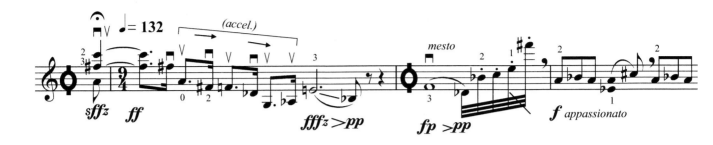

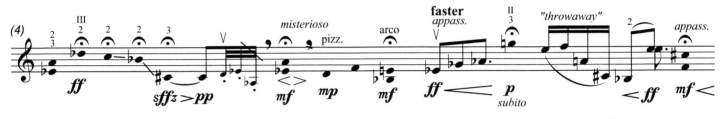

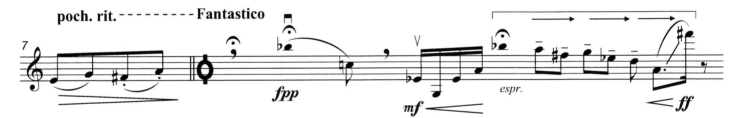

* Variations should be performed straightforwardly, "deadpan."

Var. 1
Sempre lo stesso tempo

Var. 2

Var. 3 Minore
♩ = 54

Var. 4 Majore

CADENZA
Fast

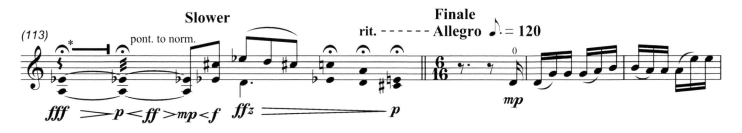

* 𝄎 = pressure bow

(La demoiselle s'eloigne. Le nain furieux.)

accelerando poco a poco al fine →

cresc. poco a poco

ancora accel.

As fast as possible

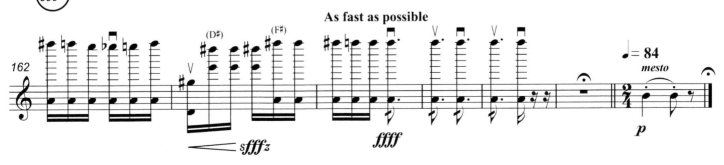

4. The Abandoned Ferryboat

♪ = **90** *Faraway; disembodied, floating, half-submerged*

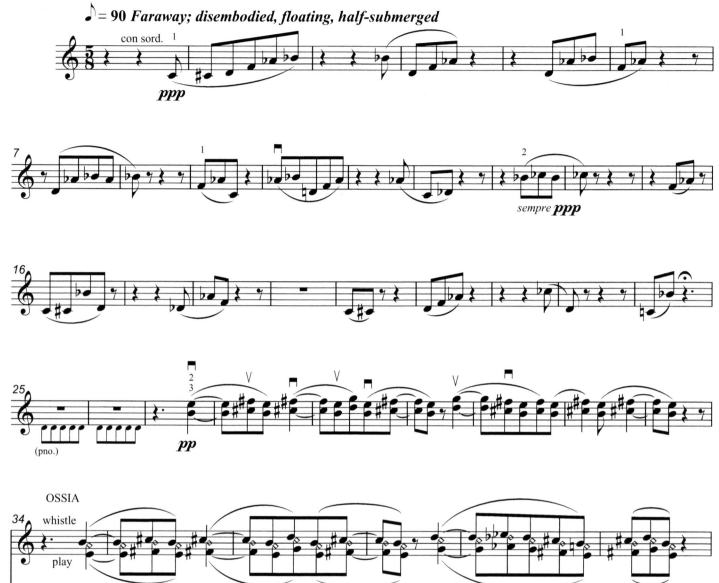

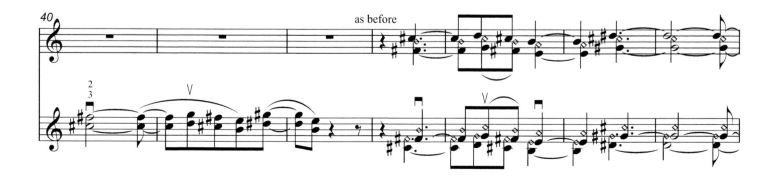

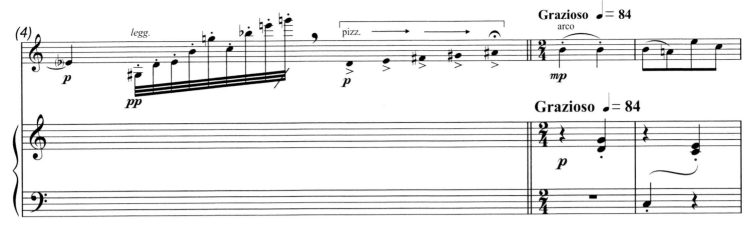

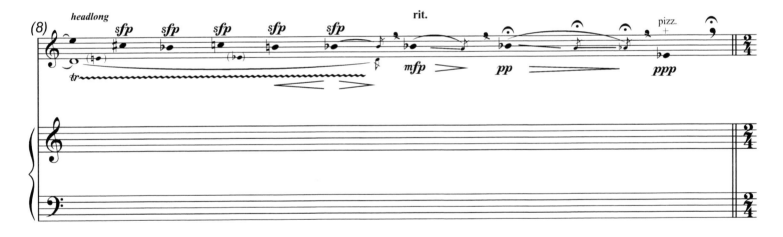

* Variations should be performed straightforwardly, "deadpan."

segue between variations

Var. 1
Sempre lo stesso tempo

Var. 2

Var. 3 Minore

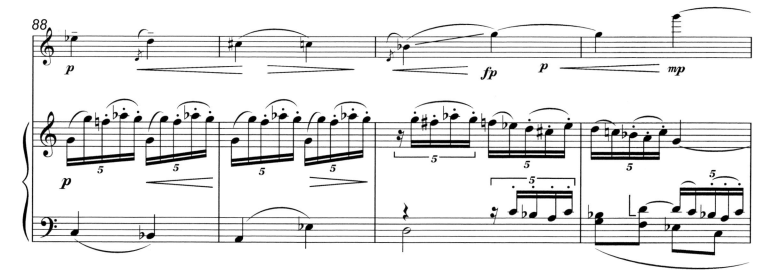

Var. 4 Majore

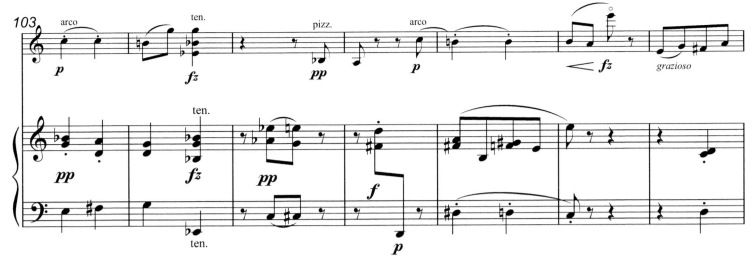

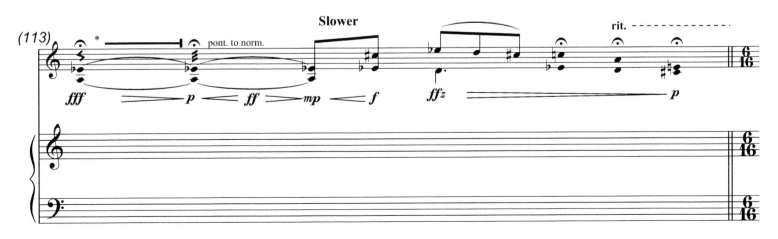

* ⚡ = pressure bow

Finale

(La demoiselle s'eloigne. Le nain furieux.)

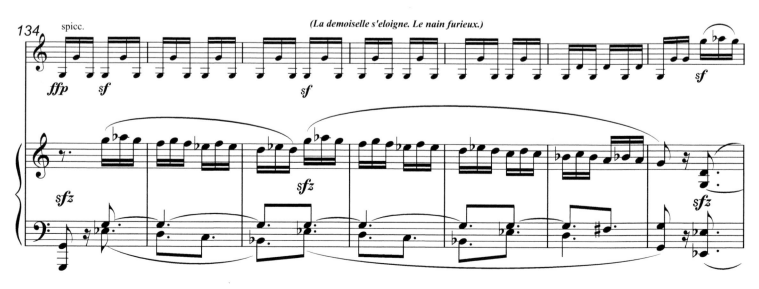

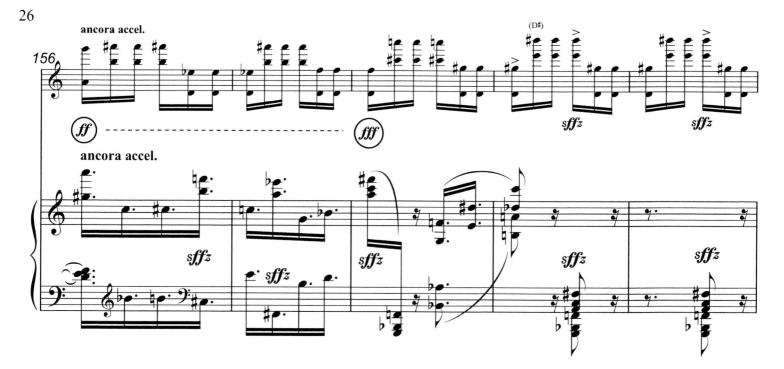

Nov. 7, 1972
N.Y.C.

4. The Abandoned Ferryboat

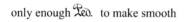
only enough Ped. to make smooth

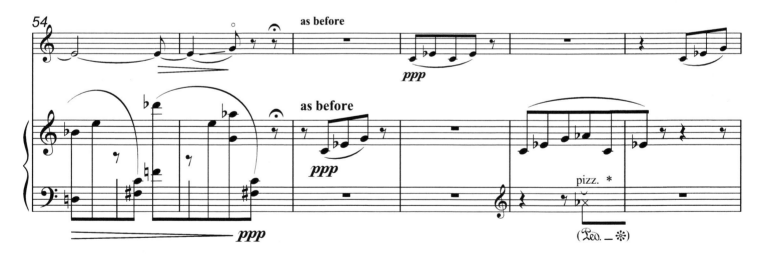

* ⌣ = with nail. Tail after note shows the length of the "touches" of pedal needed to sustain the plucked notes.

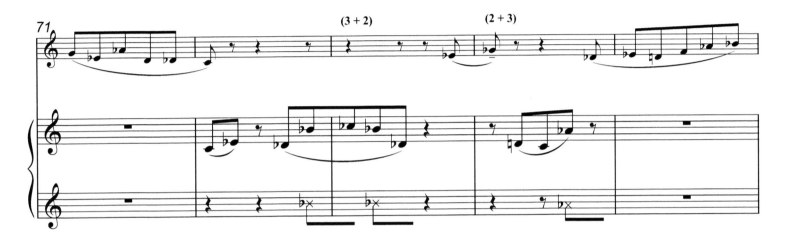

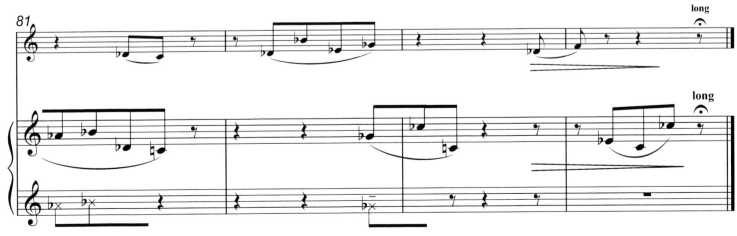

Nov. 17, 1972
N.Y.C.

GLOSSARY

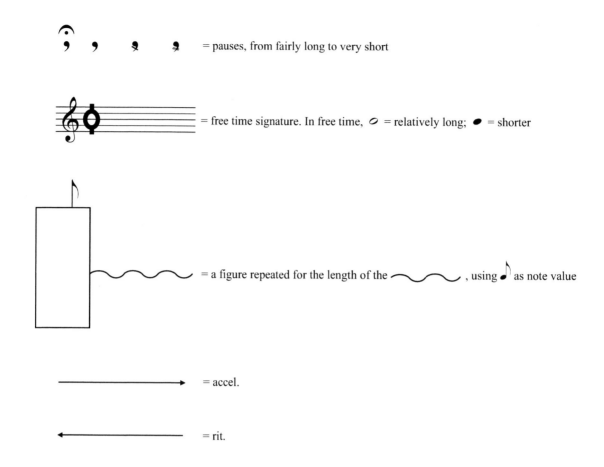

= pauses, from fairly long to very short

= free time signature. In free time, $\circ$ = relatively long; $\bullet$ = shorter

= a figure repeated for the length of the ⌣⌣ , using ♪ as note value

= accel.

= rit.

Accidentals obtain throughout a beamed group. Unbeamed notes continue the same accidental until interrupted by another note or rest. (Additional courtesy accidentals are given to ensure clarity.) In music with key signature, traditional rules apply.

NB - There are slight differences in the violin part between the single part and the violin part in the score. What is in the score represents the composer's intentions. However, the composer approves, with thanks, the editorial suggestions in the violin part by Philip Ficsor.

W.B.